# Grave Hunting - Tips and Tales

by

Martin and Claire Nicholson

The photo on the front cover is of Barnoon Cemetery, St Ives, Cornwall

# Introduction

We began our survey of graveyards and cemeteries in 2008, when we lived in Northamptonshire. We moved to Shropshire in 2010. Most of the sites we have visited have been close to our homes, but we have also visited churches and cemeteries when we have been in other parts of the country, ranging from Cornwall to the Isle of Skye, and from Aberystwyth to Suffolk. We have even visited overseas cemeteries when we have been on holiday. We have visited sites in towns, villages and in totally isolated locations, but have not visited many cemeteries in large cities.

Our favourite type of day out takes us along winding country lanes to peaceful and scenic rural churches, with no traffic noise, just sheep, cattle and birdsong. What could be nicer on a sunny day?

Gravestones can be revealing sources of social history. Modern medicine has had an enormous impact on child mortality and on lifespan. We have found few memorials to centenarians who died prior to the middle of the twentieth century, but we have found many more from the last few decades. Young women are over-represented in older graveyards due to the hazards of childbirth – one stone lamented a death due to "the agonizeing pains of childbed", and many families lost children, sometimes as many as ten over two decades, while others lost several in just a few days due to infectious diseases that are now rarely seen.

In coastal towns, the dangers of life at sea are very apparent in the tales told of drownings and lost ships, in peacetime as well as in wartime. Similarly, before the introduction of health and safety legislation, in coal-mining areas it is shocking to read of so many deaths in colliery accidents.

How many people do you know now who pursue the occupation of lion tamer, or soap boiler and tallow chandler? How many ways are there of expressing "died"? We have seen "Gone fishing", "Sublunary destiny ended", "Received marching orders", "Promoted to Glory", "Reached the end of the line" and many others.

We are usually on our own, but on some trips we had help from our younger daughter, from siblings from both sides of the family and also, in Cornwall, from a good friend. We find that other people are happy to join us for a day to see what we get up to, but they probably go home and laugh about our dedication!

In eight years we have found gravestones recording exactly 1000 centenarians, of whom 83% are female, and we have had 931 successful visits. We originally went out just for half-days, but now that we have to drive further to find "new" churches we go out for the whole day.

We have included an appendix giving the location of every grave mentioned here, and there is a picture of every one on our website www.grave-mistakes.info.

## Why go grave hunting?

We go grave-hunting because we never know what we will find. Occasionally a study has been made of a single churchyard by an enthusiastic local person, but no-one seems to have made a study of the burial sites across a wider area. There is no way to "look up" churchyards in advance to find out whether there are any unusual gravestones there because that information is simply not available.

Many people enjoy visiting graveyards and cemeteries, and they have a variety of reasons for that. Some people are looking for the graves of family members. We have been excited to find our own relatives' graves in Wolverhampton, in Barnsley and in Suffolk after making special trips there, and even went on a package holiday to the First World War battlefields to find the name of a great-uncle on one of the memorials to the many missing soldiers. There are records of the occupants of all graves in churchyards and cemeteries, and it is possible to find the exact location of a particular grave prior to visiting the site. However, many graves are not marked by any sort of headstone; even so, visitors may still be able to locate the exact position of the grave sought by reference to neighbouring gravestones.

Other cemetery visitors are looking for the burial plot of a famous or well-known person. Again, cemetery record offices will be able to assist. In some cases the noticeboard by the entrance of the cemetery may provide directions to such notable graves. We have found a number of graves of well-known people by chance, ranging from John Betjeman to "Capability" Brown to the infamous Kray twins.

The designs of gravestones and monuments to the dead are enormously varied. Some people are fascinated by such variety, with particular designs and materials used often restricted to quite small localities, or the product of individual notable stonemasons. Others are interested in particular manufacturers of headstones, which may have been sold all over the country. The statuary in cemeteries can be wonderful. We note the variability of longevity of particular materials – slate is the very best, while some types of sandstone erode quickly.

Have you ever spent time in an old cemetery reading the inscriptions on the old gravestones? It can be a fascinating exercise to read the often elaborate epitaphs, verses, biblical quotations and descriptions of the virtues (or sometimes otherwise!) of the deceased. We have found several versions of an epitaph to blacksmiths, and also of another epitaph that laments the inability of physicians to help the afflicted. There is a huge variety of inscription fonts. Some gravestone inscriptions are very short, while others are of great length and must have taken the monumental mason a long time to create, at considerable expense to the family of the deceased.

Sometimes we spot spelling mistakes on gravestones. At one small cemetery we met a gentleman who had travelled some distance to visit the recent grave of his wife. He was most upset that her name had been spelled wrongly. He had been assured by the monumental mason who had made the stone for him that it would be put right, but it was still incorrect. We do hope that he eventually got the headstone made properly.

We visit cemeteries and churchyards to look for gravestones that are out of the ordinary. Most gravestones are only of interest to the families of the deceased. They only have the name of the deceased and his/her immediate family, and the dates of birth and death. These account for probably well over 99% of all gravestones. The other tiny percentage are the ones that we look for. The deceased might have lived to be over 100 years old, or the headstone gives details of the cause of death, whether from illness, or accident at work or leisure. There may be details of military service. Other details might be about the deceased's interests, work occupation, marital history, details of his or her children (many of whom may have died in infancy), or there may be spelling or grammatical errors made by the stonemason who engraved the inscription. These sorts of headstones will rarely be noted in the records or in any publications about the church or cemetery.

Some people like to take on the task of recording all the inscriptions of the headstones in their local cemetery. For a large site this is a formidable task. The development of the digital camera has made this more feasible now than it would have been in the past. Some of these studies have been made available either in print or more recently online.

We make all our discoveries available on our own website www.grave-mistakes.info, and we would encourage other people to follow suit. They can make use of groups such as Facebook special-interest groups, and there are other family history groups that would welcome relevant material.

## How to hunt for gravestones safely.

Do not visit cemeteries or churchyards on your own. In large town cemeteries that are still being used for new burials there would probably never be a problem because there are nearly always other people visiting the site, but old graveyards that are no longer being used for new burials may be badly maintained, and quite hazardous to walk around. You do need to be quite physically fit and agile. The vegetation may be rampant, memorials may be decaying and in danger of collapse, and the ground surface may be very uneven. Some old urban graveyards may also be favoured by the "undesirable" members of the community who are best avoided.

In rural areas, the parish church may be very isolated. We may visit eight or ten small country churches in a day and not encounter a single other person, though Easter Monday 2015 was such a beautiful warm sunny day that this general observation was confounded – we met more people on one outing than we normally meet on ten trips!

Some churchyards have areas that are not maintained, with overgrown vegetation, or there may be broken kerbstones surrounding the graves that are hidden by long grass and lying in wait to trip the unwary grave-hunter. There may be very uneven ground, there may be molehills to trip on, and some graves subside leaving large depressions or visible holes in the ground. If you visit such a site alone, and then fall in the furthermost corner and break your leg or knock yourself out, there may be no other visitor to come to your rescue. A local person might say "I saw that blue car there five days ago on Monday, and it is still there today, I wonder why." No-one may have reason to go behind the church for weeks, especially in winter, so be warned!

Do wear suitable footwear, to cope with ground unevenness and mud. Long grass can be very wet even in the summer.

Do take a mobile phone with you, though it will not necessarily work in some rural areas.

## When to go grave-hunting.

Do choose a nice sunny day.  If you take photographs of churches, cemeteries or individual gravestones, they will look much better on a nice day.  We are perhaps unusual in spending whole days on our grave-hunting trips, but we rarely venture out in the winter because the days are too short, and light for photographs can be difficult.  However middle-of-the-day trips on a sunny crisp winter day can still be very successful.

We do not usually go out on Sundays when church services are likely to be taking place, with resulting car-parking difficulty, and no opportunity to go into the church to look for interior memorials and monuments.

We like to look round graveyards even when we are on holiday, and on those occasions you just have to accept the weather on the day.  At one lovely coastal cemetery the sun was shining, but just out to sea there was clearly a band of rain.  For a while it seemed to move parallel to the coast, but sure enough, it did eventually move over us before we had finished our survey.  We were thankful for the umbrellas that we fetched from the car.  We have also had to dash for the car during other showers, and we afterwards find that the rain on the gravestones does not always enhance the legibility of the inscriptions.

Graveyard visits do not have to be planned – if you find yourself with a bit of spare time anywhere in the country, there is usually a nearby church!

## How to find the grave that you want.

If you are looking for a specific grave in a large cemetery or churchyard, the best plan is to contact the cemetery office or the vicar of the church in advance of your visit.  They maintain records of all burials and may send you a plan of the site with relevant grave number.  Occasionally we have been approached by another visitor who asks us if we know where the grave of a particular named person is.  We explain what we are doing, and then watch the person wandering in an unsystematic way and haphazard round the site.

Many graves are not marked with a headstone.  This may be because the family of the deceased chose not to erect a headstone, or could not afford to.  Alternatively old gravestones may become unsafe and have been removed, or the church authorities may have moved old gravestones to facilitate mowing of the grass.  Some of these headstones may have been re-erected in neat rows, or against the perimeter wall of the site, but sadly others are just piled up or even used as paving stones.

We search for unusual gravestones, and the only way to find them is to read every inscription. We never know in advance what we are going to find. The only way to do this is to survey the whole site systematically. If it is a large urban cemetery there is often a map at the entrance. We find it helpful to sketch a copy of this, and to cross off each area as we survey it. We walk up and down the rows, and if the gravestones all face in the same direction we can often survey two rows in one pass. It becomes more awkward if the gravestones do not all face in the same direction.

Some visits result in many more interesting "finds" than others. In one recent visit to a large modern urban cemetery we timed our survey. We concluded that it had taken us about 7 man-hours to survey between 8,000 and 10,000 gravestones – this works out at about 20 per minute. This cemetery had neat regular rows on well-mown flat ground. In contrast, overgrown old cemeteries are far, far slower than this, without taking into account driving time between well-scattered rural churches.

We have sometimes been asked whether we are looking for a grave of a relative, and sometimes the questioner has been willing to direct us to the records inside the church. We explain that no, we are just looking for unusual gravestones, and find that the person is often quite interested in what we are doing. We have some business cards with our website details that we often hand to people.

Sometimes we meet stonemasons erecting new headstones, or workmen who are responsible for the maintenance of the cemetery. They are often particularly knowledgeable about "their" cemetery and will tell us about gravestones of interest there, and on more than one occasion have already discovered our website on the internet. We found one gravestone that recorded that the occupant was the former cemetery keeper, and that he had actually died in "his" cemetery and was subsequently buried there. Not everyone dies in bed when old or ill – one young lad died at his school desk, a church organist died at his post in church, and another young woman actually "died suddenly in this chapel during service"! In contrast, we were dismayed to find a memorial that noted death due to a "bleeding cancer" and another that was due to "confluent smallpox".

A lot of old rural churches have new graveyard areas which might be across the road or over the wall or through that narrow little gate, so do be nosy and have a good look round to ensure you do not miss anything.

Always go to the far corner of the churchyard or cemetery to look at the last isolated headstone – it might prove to be the highlight discovery of the day!

## Photograph the gravestones you have discovered.

We recommend using a good-quality camera. We use a digital SLR camera, and for most pictures the auto facility produces very good results. The exceptions are difficult lighting conditions. If the face of the headstone is in shade with bright light behind it, it can be helpful to use the manual setting on the camera to increase the exposure of the picture, or if the headstone is in deep shade under a tree use of flash can be a good idea. Make sure that you have plenty of battery power.

Some modern gravestones are shiny, which can act like a mirror, with the unfortunate result that there can be a clear reflection of the photographer in the picture! We do not go out armed with special equipment to deal with this problem, but it has been suggested to us that the photographer should don a black tent with a hole for the camera to poke through! A simpler remedy can be to take the photograph from a slightly offset position.

The engraving on gravestones can be significantly easier to read when it is enhanced by sunlight to the side. We made a special visit to one near our home because it was quite badly eroded and difficult to read. At about 5 p.m. the sun just began to strike the face of the stone and highlight the inscription. The epitaph was then at its most readable – what dedication to our hobby!

Do set the clock on your camera if possible – see our later advice on record-keeping.

## Should you clean the gravestones?

We have seen discussions of graveyard etiquette that advise cleaning gravestones with materials such as brushes, sponges, WD-40 (for metal surfaces), and paper towels.

We would emphatically disagree with this. The gravestones are not your property, and should be left as you find them. It is perfectly acceptable to use your hand to sweep off dead leaves or stray grass clippings, or to break off a weed or two that is growing up in front of the gravestone, but that is all.

You would not want an unknown person to "clean" your car with unknown materials without your permission, and the same applies to gravestones. The surfaces of many old gravestones are eroding and deteriorating, and any aggressive and unauthorised "cleaning" you apply may only accelerate the process. Do not do it.

## Keeping records during your graveyard visits.

We take a notebook with us to record the name of the church or cemetery and its location. We set the time on the clock on the camera, and we record the time when we are at each site to make it easier to identify the photographs afterwards. If there is anything else that we wish to remember about the site, such as being surprised by a fox, or a chat with a man over a wall, or the standard of maintenance of the area, we write it down. Do remember to take a general photograph of the church itself or of the cemetery to "set the scene" for your gravestones.

## Do look inside the church.

When we began our grave-hunting we did not often go inside the churches. More recently we have always tried the church door handle, and have been astounded by the quality of some memorials and monuments inside quite modest small churches.

Sometimes the door is locked, but there may be a notice giving details of the key-holder. We have found keys with near neighbours, or hanging behind the church notice board, and on several occasions asking a nearby person has been productive.

We particularly wanted to see one interior monument, but the church was locked, with no such notice. We made a subsequent visit, and were pleased to find new details inside the porch. We telephoned the number given when we were about 30 minutes driving time away on our way home later that day, and were rewarded with the key-holder waiting for us, and a spectacular monument to a lady and her infant son. Persistence can pay off!

Urban churches are more often kept locked for security reasons, and we do notice that some of them are now being used for other community reasons such as cafes or art galleries.

Many churches offer publications for sale that describe the architecture of the church, its stained glass, the font, the lectern, the local benefactors, the clerical incumbents or other features of interest. Some will give details of particular interior monuments, but very few give much detail about the graveyard outside, unless there is someone famous buried there. It is worth taking a small amount of cash to pay for these small booklets. This history is often available online. There are also continuing projects to make parish registers available online.

If the vicar is at his church, it is polite to ask his permission for interior photography. We have never been refused permission, and normally find that the vicars are pleased to speak to anyone who has an interest in their church. At some large urban churches or cathedrals that are popular with tourists you may be asked to pay a small sum for a photography permit.

## Be polite and respectful.

If there are mourners at a burial ceremony it is clearly not appropriate to try to survey the gravestones close to them. You would either have to revisit on another day, or wait until they had dispersed. The same applies to individuals who are visiting a grave of a family member – sometimes it is apparent that they are very upset.

At large urban cemeteries it is usually possible to drive in, and there is usually an obvious area designated for parking. Do not take your car over grass just to minimise walking distance!

On one occasion we arrived at a village church. There were quite a lot of people and cars nearby, and the people soon disappeared into the village hall across the road from the church. We began our survey, and were somewhat disconcerted to see an open grave, with the newly deposited coffin inside it. A lady nearby asked us if we were mourners and if we had been at the funeral that had just taken place, but we assured her that we were not mourners, just visitors!

If the noticeboard at the entrance instructs that dogs should not be taken into the churchyard or cemetery, please abide by the request.

On one memorable occasion in a town cemetery we were looking at a recent grave of a young man that was very elaborate and ostentatious. We personally thought that it was hideous, until a young woman pulled up in her car behind us. The grave was that of her brother, killed in a car accident. We did our best to tell her that we were "admiring the grave", and that it was very impressive and eye-catching. We hope that she believed us!

On another occasion at a peaceful country church we sat on a bench to eat our lunch, and admired the nearby grave. As we went back to our car, two more people arrived. We had a chat and it transpired that we had been sitting by their son's grave, sited so that they could see it from their home some distance away.

We have had to move seats when a burial party arrived – it might not be considered respectful to continue eating our sandwiches as the coffin-bearers and mourners walked round us!

In general we do not take photographs of modern gravestones of babies. We feel that the loss of a baby is such a personal tragedy for the family that it is not appropriate to use them for our website.

### Churchyard maintenance.

The maintenance of graveyards and cemeteries is a big task. In large urban cemeteries it is usually the responsibility of the local council, and they often do a very good job. However we well remember one winter-time visit to an urban cemetery where there was a group of five council workmen. At lunchtime we sat in our car to eat our sandwiches, and were "entertained" by the men who were occupied on the verges surrounding the car park area. It seemed that at any one moment only one man was very slowly doing any work, while the other four leaned on their tools and watched and talked. Then another of the group took over for a few minutes. The overall work rate was pitiful.

We returned home and sent an email message to the responsible department of the local council describing our observations, and how we would not want to be tax payers of that area giving pay to such idle men. Soon afterwards we were gratified to receive a reply thanking us for our message and assuring us that the men had been spoken to, and their practice of working in groups changed. The tax payers of that town should be grateful to us!

We are dismayed when we find examples of neglect or disrespect in churchyards. Sometimes old or broken gravestones are just piled up as rubbish in a corner. The worst example of disrespect we have found was the use of old gravestones to surround and support the rubbish heap where grass cuttings were dumped. Some of those stones were still legible!

The maintenance of smaller churchyards is often undertaken by volunteers. In some of them areas of older gravestones are set aside as "nature reserves". In the summer months they quickly become very overgrown, and it is impossible to get safely to the gravestones to read them, which is frustrating for us. When we do meet people mowing grass or looking after flowerbeds we always compliment them on their work. Everyone likes to know that their work is appreciated, so be nice to the volunteers.

## How do I find every church?

In many rural areas there is no public transport, or maybe only one bus a week, so it is impossible to visit churches there without your own transport. The roads are frequently just single-track lanes so the driver also needs to be competent at reversing when another vehicle is approaching.

We find that Philips Street Atlases, which are published for every county, are ideal for grave-hunting. Every church is marked with a cross, and every cemetery is marked "Cemy". The maps are large scale, so we mark every church after we have visited it, and after we have visited every church on a page we mark off that page on the index page at the front of the atlas.

When we are ready for our next trip it is an easy matter to sort out which map pages have been "done" and where to head to next.

Sometimes we look at online aerial maps before our visit. It is then possible to eliminate some urban churches which are clearly modern or which do not have a graveyard. A road named "Church Lane" or "St. Mary Street" is a good clue to a nearby parish church with a graveyard.

However there is no way of distinguishing between large or small churches, or "tin hut" chapels, or those which have been converted into dwellings just by looking at the map. Sometimes churches marked on the map have just vanished!

We note that when a village name is entered on satellite navigation devices, the church is often the point at which "You have now reached your destination."

## Survival tips!

We find that we get quite thirsty after a few hours of tramping round hundreds or thousands of gravestones, so take plenty to drink with you. It can be a good plan to have a pub lunch, but many rural pubs do not serve lunches on Mondays, so we usually take a picnic with us. It is worth remembering that many large supermarkets serve good-value meals all day – a good way to eat on the way home after a long (but hopefully exciting) day out.

The next problem is toilets! It is very rare for rural churches to have a toilet on the site, so, ladies, you have to learn not to be shy, and improvise when there is no-one looking!

We also share the driving, with one of us doing the narrow-lanes driving and parking while the other is responsible for planning the route. We each have our strengths, and find that delegation of roles works well for us. We have even established a routine in which one of us always turns to the left inside the churchyard gate, and the other turns to the right, and we meet at the back of the church.

## Potential technical disasters.

We have only had one occasion of camera breakdown – totally unpredictable. We just had to go home!

No-one should need to be reminded of the importance of computer good practice regarding keeping back-ups of all data.

It would be a totally demoralising disaster if the only record of our gravestone discoveries was lost in a house fire, for example. Therefore do not just keep the camera memory cards, or just one file copy on your computer. You have been warned!

## Publicise the results of your grave-hunts.

In modern times with the internet it is easy to share your discoveries. It does not make sense to spend a lot of time and effort in finding and photographing interesting gravestones and to then not to make your photographs publicly available. All our gravestone discoveries are on our own website www.grave-mistakes.info, and there is a picture of the site accompanying every gravestone picture.

We have a blog http://grave-mistakes.blogspot.co.uk/ in which we share our favourite discoveries, and have also published two books which are available from Amazon. They are "Discovering Gravestones", a guide to the relative rarity of different types of gravestones and their inscriptions, and "Gravestones of Shropshire", our selection of the best of the county's gravestones, written after we had visited every church and cemetery in the county, a process which took nearly 4 years.

We have recently completed our survey of all of the churches of Herefordshire, with a view to producing a similar book on that county's best gravestones, with one for Worcestershire next on our list.

We are also members of a number of Facebook groups for grave-hunters. These groups have members from all over the world, and are a simple forum for showing off pictures of what you discover to like-minded people. However we do think that there are too many groups – some people seem to start them without a sufficiently large "stock" of their own discoveries to support the group for more than a few weeks.

Contact with other grave-hunters.

If you have a specific project in mind, for example doing a complete photographic survey of one particular graveyard, it would be sensible to check beforehand that no-one has already done the same thing. Sometimes in a small church we have found a file with transcriptions of the inscriptions on the gravestones in that churchyard, but we have not yet found such a file with a photographic record. Making such a survey would not be of interest to us, because we find that the proportion of "interesting" gravestones is very low.

Our blog entries do solicit comments sometimes from viewers. Some just admire the gravestone, while others have interesting extra information about it.

One of our most memorable gravestones recorded the birth and subsequent deaths of quadruplets in the nineteenth century in a small village in Wales. An adjacent headstone also recorded the death of five year old twins of the same family, and their father, all within a month or two.  We were later informed that this very unusual event had been in the local news at the time, and that the deaths were due to typhoid.

We were also contacted by a lady who thanked us for showing the gravestone of her grandparents who had died together while their son was only a baby.  She had not known where the grave was, and was so pleased to find it.

We have a small section of our website devoted to our own family graves. During the course of his own family research a gentleman in Canada found our picture of the gravestone in Suffolk of one of our great-great-uncles, who was also one of his ancestors.  He contacted us, and also sent us online copies of some family photographs of our mutual ancestors.

On a less pleasing subject, we were telephoned by a lady who requested that we remove the picture of her family grave from our website.  Her reason was rather vague, but we complied promptly.  However she never thanked us afterwards, so we might reinstall it!

The only other request for removal was so aggressive that we ignored it. We take the view that if families choose to make their loved one's gravestone unusual by placing extra information about the deceased on it, they should not be surprised when it attracts the attention of grave-hunters.

Our own blog has up to 2000 viewers a day, and Facebook groups for grave-hunters can have over 10,000 worldwide members, so the hobby is of interest to many people. Most of the members of the Facebook groups are in the USA.  We are however surprised at how few of these people pursue the hobby actively themselves - the entries for the groups are provided by only a very small proportion of the members. We also note that very few of the members seem to offer photographs of unusual inscriptions on gravestones – almost all the postings (except ours) are of eye-catching statuary or unusual designs that can be spotted from a distance.

Please, if you put postings of your gravestone discoveries on the internet, do say where they are.  Many wonderful pictures give no indication of where they were taken, which seems so thoughtless.

## What else have we learned?

We are not religious, so we have surprised ourselves by getting a lot of pleasure from our church visits. We have also learned a lot about the churches themselves. We are gradually acquiring a selection of "churches" books, and now know what a piscina is, we recognise a sedila and a baldacino, and have committed the phrase "sheela-na-gig" to memory. Norman arches are very distinctive, and we now know how to recognise a stained glass window made by the Kempe studio (look for a small wheatsheaf in the lower left hand corner).

We are sometimes asked if we find graveyards eerie or spooky. No, we do not. However there was once a young man near a cemetery entrance who seemed to disappear remarkably suddenly.....!

We have learned that slate is the most durable material for gravestones. Inscriptions that are over 200 years old are as legible as the day they were engraved. In contrast we would like to issue a plea for families to not choose gold lettering on speckled headstones – they are unreadable in very few years.

## Research

Many gravestones offer information that can be expanded upon with a few minutes research at home on the internet. Genealogy is a popular hobby with both magazines and websites available to help. We have been excited to find a few old gravestones of our own families, and have included them in separate pages on our website, and also have a page devoted to one particular family surname. The "finds" for that page seem to be concentrated in the Midlands, with almost none in other parts of the country, which is interesting.

Military disasters and losses, or industrial accidents are well documented on the internet, as are famous people or any event that may have been reported in the press at the time.

## Unexpected pleasures (and disappointments).

It is lovely to drive down a winding lane that has grass growing in the middle (so obviously not subject to much traffic!) and find a gem of a church. Sometimes there are a few houses or farms, other times the church is in splendid isolation and we wonder why it was built there and where the former and present congregations live.

We have found sheep and hens in churchyards doing their bit in keeping the grass down, (do not forget to leave gates closed if that is how you find them) and have admired cattle, horses, and wonderful views. We have been surprised by foxes and rabbits which have leaped out in front of us, we have seen lots of squirrels, nearly run over hundreds of pheasants, we have listened to the screeches of a white pheasant high up in a conifer tree, we have stroked many cats that patrol cemeteries, and seen wonderful displays of snowdrops, primroses, daffodils, and crocuses in spring.

We have resigned ourselves to never having a clean car – it is impossible to drive far down country lanes without encountering mud. Perhaps if you are car-proud, rural grave-hunting is not the hobby for you! Occasionally we have had to "shoo" cattle out of the way!

We are pleased to find old gravestones that have obviously been cleaned or refurbished, and dismayed to find overgrown graves with neglected gravestones that state that the deceased is "Gone but not forgotten". Clearly no longer true!

The Commonwealth War Graves Commission has areas in many large urban cemeteries that are beautifully maintained, but many churches also have a handful of scattered CWGC gravestones that are really dirty, which is disappointing. We have talked to two gardeners who take great pride in their maintenance of the CWGC graves, and who are very knowledgeable about the individuals interred there.

It can be a mistake to think that the small church at which you have just arrived will not contain anything special. Even small rural churches can contain some fantastic memorials and tombs that would not be out of place in a truly grand large church. We have often walked into an unremarkable church and said "Wow, look at that!" on finding a wonderful effigy or wall monument that may be 800 or 900 years old. The unexpected finds are part of what we enjoy in our hobby.

We do not always find gravestones worth photographing (in our view) at all the churches we visit. Sometimes it is apparent as soon as we drive up that this "church" is a small chapel with no surrounding graveyard. In Wales particularly it can be frustrating to drive miles along lanes to find that the target "church" is a corrugated iron tin chapel for The Primitive Methodists, with no graveyard.

Modern cemeteries are easy to survey – they are well maintained, and the gravestones are laid out in tidy rows. They contain more centenarians, but older churchyards which are more challenging to survey produce more interesting discoveries.

Some days we find a lovely selection of unusual gravestones, and on other days we visit a number of churches and find very few of note – that is part of the fun of the chase! Viewers of our website or blog might get the misleading impression that it is easy to find unusual gravestones because we have found so many. It is not! It takes a lot of time, a lot of physical effort to walk past every single gravestone to read it (but it is good exercise), a lot of mileage (2500 miles this year) with significant cost, but we enjoy it! However, we do find it disappointing that many people say that they like the pictures that we place on the internet, but apparently want only free entertainment because they do not support us by paying a small sum to buy one of our books.

### These are gravestones, but you have to laugh sometimes.....!

A favourite message from a member of a Facebook grave-hunting group concerned the dearth of images of graves in South Dakota. Why did we not show more graves in her state? Well, actually we live the other side of the Atlantic Ocean! If she lives in South Dakota she can go out and find them for herself!

We are surprised at the errors we find on gravestones, including obvious alterations of the name of the deceased! Sometimes the alteration makes it impossible to work out what is the correct name - the same applies to the age of the deceased.

We have found "tradgically", "shaddows", "thier", "rememberance", "accidently", "farther", lots of apostrophes incorrectly placed, and have been left wondering why the families accepted headstones with obvious errors. On very old stones spelling was variable, so words like "Physician" appear with various spellings.

One error was memorable because it was the first word at the top of an old gravestone. In very large fancy script there was the word "Sacerd"! Another gravestone made us wonder, because the deceased had been "killed by lightning after preaching"!

We have smiled at some of the phrases on modern gravestones. We have seen "Now sweeping chimney's in heaven" (note the apostrophe!),

"The lady with the dog", "A nice cup of tea please", and "Make em laugh Dave".

Amusing for other reasons are gravestones such as that for "Ma and Conk" and for "Bill". These bore no other inscription at all, so in a few years no-one will know who the deceased was.

And finally, on a much sadder note, some gravestones record deaths that happened in attempts to rescue others from drowning, and, bizarrely, one person was killed with a cartwheel.

## Review of our year of 2015.

We have already visited all the churches within about a 50-mile radius of our home, so in 2015 we had to drive for over an hour to reach "new" ones. We have visited Herefordshire, (and have now been to every church or cemetery in that county), Worcestershire, Staffordshire, and a few sites in other counties. We have had 19 single days out from home, and two short breaks, in Lincolnshire to visit friends, and in Cambridgeshire for a family party, which we also used as an opportunity to make some church visits. We made a trip to the battlefields of the First World War and enjoyed visits to a number of the Commonwealth War Graves Commission cemeteries and memorials there.

We made 204 successful visits, and 55 visits where we did not find any graves that we deemed worth photographing. We drove over 2500 miles.

A highlight of 2015 was finding a cadaver tomb from the fifteenth century in one church, and a gravestone that told of the death of three boys when a barn fell down. They were taking shelter there during a "violent hurricane" in 1877.

## More projects.

In Shropshire we are not far from the Welsh border, so we have visited quite a lot of Welsh churches. However, as the Welsh language is used on many Welsh gravestones, we cannot understand them and have no way of knowing whether the inscription is describing some really dramatic cause of death.

There is therefore an opportunity for a Welsh-speaker to do the same sort of project as ours, but over the border in Wales.

We try to go inside the churches, and love finding dramatic monuments there, but the core purpose of our survey is the gravestones outside. We do take some interior photographs, but we would encourage others to take that project more seriously. Individual church guidebooks often describe their principal monuments, but there are no studies (as far as we can find) that cover all the interior memorials in all the churches over a wide area. Many of these monuments are very large, and cataloguing them would be a lovely project for a keen photographer with sophisticated lighting equipment.

## Conclusion.

We hope we have sparked some enthusiasm in you. Under some trees at one graveyard we were pleased to spot a gravestone that mentioned the Zulu War battle at Isandlwana. The inscription was quite dirty and eroded, but we managed to get a readable photograph. At home later, doing some research into the individual named, we found another picture of the same gravestone, but in much better condition than that in which we had found it. This demonstrates well how the decay of gravestones is a continuing process. The choice of material is key – slate lasts for ever, while softer stones erode and flake away quite quickly. We have even found a couple of sandstone gravestones that had eroded so much that there was a hole through the middle! Gravestones are a valuable social history resource, but many have already been lost for ever.

Therefore, don't delay, go out exploring today. That wonderful old gravestone might not still be there next year, or even next week!

And finally – can you find a churchyard memorial stone more exciting than one telling the story of a lady who committed infanticide, was tried for the crime, and was executed just a few days after the trial!

# Appendix

| | |
|---|---|
| Agonizeing pains of childbed | St. Stephen, Old Radnor, Powys |
| Ten children died | St. Giles, Northampton, Northamptonshire |
| Four children in four days | St. David, Llanarth, Ceredigion |
| Lost at sea | Aberystwyth Cemetery, Ceredigion |
| Colliery accidents | Barnsley Cemetery, South Yorkshire |
| Lion tamer | St. Philip, Penn Fields, Wolverhampton |
| Soap boiler and tallow chandler | St Michael and All Angels, Ledbury, Herefordshire |
| Gone fishing | Hay on Wye Cemetery, Powys |
| Sublunary destiny ended | Holy Trinity, Dawley, Shropshire |
| Received marching orders | Bromyard Cemetery, Herefordshire |
| Promoted to Glory | Histon and Impington Cemetery, Cambridgeshire |
| Reached the end of the line | St. Bartholomew, Tardebigge, Worcestershire |
| John Betjeman | St. Enodoc, Trebetherick, Cornwall |
| "Capability" Brown | St. Peter and St. Paul, Fenstanton, Cambridgeshire |
| Kray twins | Chingford Mount Cemetery, North London |
| Blacksmith's epitaph | St. Nicholas, South Kilworth, Leicestershire |
| Physicians | St Lawrence, Gnosall, Staffordshire |
| Cemetery keeper | Kenilworth Cemetery, Warwickshire |
| At school desk | St. Michael and All Angels, Kerry, Powys |
| Organist at his post | St. Chad, Hanmer, Wrexham |
| During chapel service | Prees Green Methodist Church, Shropshire |
| Bleeding cancer | All Saints, Long Whatton, Leicestershire |
| Confluent smallpox | St. Endelienta, St. Endellion, Cornwall |
| Sun highlights inscription | St. Lawrence, Church Stretton, Shropshire |
| Lady and infant | St. Mary, Hope under Dinmore, Herefordshire |
| Quadruplets | Ysbyty Cwnfyn, near Devils's Bridge, Ceredigion |
| Tradgically | All Saints, Harborough Magna, Warwickshire |
| Shaddows | Welford Road Cemetery, Leicester, Leicestershire |
| Thier | Merridale Cemetery, Wolverhampton |

| | |
|---|---|
| Rememberance | Shobdon Cemetery, Herefordshire |
| Accidently | St. James the Great, Cradley, Herefordshire |
| Farther | All Saints, Madeley, Staffordshire |
| Sacerd | St. James the Great, Colwall, Herefordshire |
| Killed by lightning | Milverton Cemetery, Warwick, Warwickshire |
| Now sweeping chimney's | St. Bartholomew, Holmer, Herefordshire |
| The lady with the dog | St. Dubricius, Whitchurch, Herefordshire |
| A nice cup of tea please | Burton Latimer Cemetery, Northamptonshire |
| Make em laugh Dave | Stafford Crematorium, Staffordshire |
| Ma and Conk | Kingsland Cemetery, Shrewsbury, Shropshire |
| Bill | Oswestry Cemetery, Shropshire |
| Attempted rescue | Bransford Cemetery, Bransford, Worcestershire |
| Cartwheel | St. Madron, Madron, Cornwall |
| Cadaver tomb | St. Vigor's with All Saints, Fulbourn, Cambridgeshire |
| Barn fell down | Nativity of the Blessed Virgin Mary, Ringstead, Northamptonshire |
| Isandlwana | St Tetha, Teath, Cornwall |
| Hole in gravestone | St. Michael and All Angels, Stourport-on-Severn, Worcestershire |
| Execution | St. Andrew, Presteigne, Powys |

# By the same author and available from Amazon

## The Grave Hunters Series

Gravestones of Shropshire

Unusual Gravestones

Gravestones of Herefordshire (due early 2016)

## County Catalogue of Unusual War Graves and Memorials

Volume 1 – Shropshire

Volume 2 – Worcestershire

Volume 3 – Herefordshire

Volume 4 – Staffordshire (due autumn 2015)

## Unusual Commonwealth War Graves and Memorials

Volume 1 – United Kingdom

Volume 2 – Belgium (due autumn 2015)

Volume 3 – France (due autumn 2015)

## The Western Front Series

The Arras War Graves and Memorials

The Menin Gate Memorial

Thiepval War Graves and Memorials

Tyne Cot War Graves and Memorials

14225754R00015

Printed in Great Britain
by Amazon.co.uk, Ltd.,
Marston Gate.